THE LIGHT OF EVENING

The Light of Evening

meditations
ON GROWING
IN OLD AGE

Gunilla Norris

twentythirdpublications.com

Twenty-Third Publications
One Montauk Avenue, Suite 200
New London, CT 06320
(860) 437-3012 or (800) 321-0411
www.twentythirdpublications.com

Copyright © 2022 Gunilla Norris. All rights reserved. No part of this publication may be reproduced in any manner without prior written permission of the publisher. Write to the Permissions Editor.

Cover photo: stock.adobe.com / Basaltblick

ISBN: 978-1-62785-702-4
Printed in the U.S.A.

CONTENTS

Introduction 1

Waking Up 5

Our Gift 8

Taking Stock 11

Beyond Worthiness 14

Inner Healing 17

Holding 20

Letting Go 23

Letting Be 26

Forgiveness 29

Forgiving Ourselves 33

Seeing the Goodness We Are 36

Dependence 39

Dignity 42

Limitations 45

Listening 48

Time 51

Loneliness 55

Hunger 58

Old Growth 61

Called by Name 64

Curiosity 67

Memory 70

Passion 73

Loss and Absence 76

Gifting Small Things 79

Permission 82

Just 'Cause 85

Shelter 88

About Being Helpful 91

In Awe 94

Now 97

Last Words *100*

For dear friends who share the grace of growing in old age.

INTRODUCTION

Sometimes in quiet moments I wonder, how did I get to be this old? My body is slower, for certain, and my eyesight is less acute than even a year ago. It's harder to get up out of soft chairs and sofas. But, when I forget all this, along with the normal aches and pains that come with being old, I am not an octogenarian. Inside me, a world of *being* is unfolding. Being seems not to have a particular age. It is ageless.

If we elders find ourselves in nursing homes, in hospital beds and wheelchairs, it is essential to remember that a world of spiritual being is still alive inside us. We continue to grow in our later years even if we aren't very aware of it. That is a tender and holy fact. When caregivers and friends are careful about this, it is one of the most important and loving things they can give us.

I find it a wonderful and strange experience to have the feeling of lots of time now even though my life expectancy is diminished. I am sure I share that sensation with many. Perhaps that is because we elders have one foot in eternity and the other in the *agreed upon world* where everything is fast, volatile, and changing. We are in transition, asked by life to release the lived and known for something new. I want to think of this as a spiritual adventure. Could growing in our end times perhaps be the most passionately lived stage of life?

In the farmhouse on Bear Hills Road in Newtown, Connecticut, where I lived many years ago, there was an old hydrangea tree in the backyard. I feel confident when I say it was older than I am now. The tree was not tall or dramatic. It had reached its mature height, and season after season, it bloomed quietly. One could almost say it was somehow invisible because it was just *there*. That the tree seemed almost invisible was not the tree's fault. It belonged, being a tree indigenous to New England and very much itself in the farmyard.

One year it was heaped with blossoms and looked luminous, with every branch ablaze with white flowers. On moonlit nights that year, it simply glowed, luscious and somehow virginal, though it was surely a tree that had been around a long time. To me, in the moonlight it looked like a bride.

One night I heard a strange sound. It was a crack…almost like a pistol shot or the sound of sharp, electric thunder. There was no storm outside. I listened carefully, but no more sounds came. I fell asleep, confident that all was as it should be.

It was as it should be, but not as I wanted it to be. When I went outside in the morning, I found the tree keeled over on the ground. The trunk had snapped in two at the base. Blossoms spread all around the gnarled trunk. The sight was beautiful and heartbreaking. I couldn't help but wonder if the old tree had exhausted itself in a last hurrah of blossoming. Perhaps it had given all it had to give. If this was true, and I think it was, the tree's ending was organic. It fell to the waiting ground.

I mourned that tree. Can you have a personal relationship with a tree? Yes, is my answer. I had not realized how much it was part of my sense of place. Its sheer being had been a reassurance to me. That last, immense blooming was a hymn.

After a few days, the tree was hauled into the back of the woodlot. It was heaped into a pile for the safe wintering of the small animals that lived back there. Whenever I walked in among the ash trees in the woodlot, I would notice what had happened to the tree. By late fall, everything was brown and gray. The tree became so much a part of the landscape that its separate self was no longer visible. It was in and with everything around it. I wonder if that is what becomes of us when we pass from this realm. Do we simply and gently become part of all that is?

For me now, that hydrangea tree is an icon for growing in my final years. I hope to blossom with passion until the last moment. Some of what is written here may seem hard to accept. I trust you will skip those parts if you need to, and yet I know that the challenges we have as we age are openings to further growth, to living fully with the truth of things as they are. The truth will make us free and resilient. Participating with both the dark and the light sides of life in our wisdom years is passionate, filled with grace and gratitude.

I hope you won't read this book from cover to cover in one sitting. It's meant to be a friend to you, not something to get through. I hope you will pick it up from time to time and read one of the meditations. If something grabs you that I've written, then please take some moments to mull it over a bit. Don't be in any hurry. Let it keep you company and infuse you with an inner knowing or with ideas that can help you think positively about your life. Maybe there will be things there that will take you more deeply into yourself, or perhaps some suggestions will appeal to you to try your hand at in the days and months ahead. There is always growing to be done, and there are valuable things we older ones can nurture and live in the light of evening.

Waking Up

I HAVE EXPERIENCED, AND YOU MUST HAVE AS WELL, THAT THERE IS MORE TO WAKING UP THAN OPENING ONE'S PHYSICAL EYES. It may not be at first light. It may be in the dark when all is quiet. Waking up in a more than physical way is about being present and aware in the here and now, whether we are wearing pajamas or dressed to the hilt.

Waking up can happen in a confrontation, a love moment, or gazing into the bathroom mirror. To be alive this very second in whatever capacity is a miracle that we often ignore. Perhaps, for some of us, with only a few years left, it is urgent to awaken in every sense of the word. It is to embrace what Rabbi Abraham Heschel affirmed: *Just to be is a blessing. Just to live is holy.*

I believe that when we awaken in this way, we awaken into reverence and the recognition that everything around us is holy in some way. With awakened eyes, even an ordinary day can be entered with renewed presence. This day will never happen again, nor will the way we live it and love it. This is not an occasion for lament but for deepening participation in the given. Inner and outer worlds can meet. Daily, something of beauty, tenderness, understanding, and gratitude can be lived and shared. Then, even if we wake at night or are in a metaphorical darkness, *there*, for the having, is the gift of being alive even when we feel some fear now and then.

No one can live for us. Our lives can blossom with meaning only if we receive the gift of our remaining time. As our lives round toward their natural ending, we tend to have more time to reflect. The insistence of tasks to be done is not as strong. We can, in a way that we perhaps never could before, think of it as a found generosity of hours to spend in what is familiar and is yet there to be rediscovered in new ways. A day can be tasted, touched and felt, heard, seen, and smelled. To awaken this way is to sense and reverence with all our faculties the wonder of simply being.

afterthoughts

It's easy to be philosophical and grateful when things are relatively benign. But to awaken with pain, with fear, or with a sense of helplessness that sometimes comes with growing older is another matter. With the awareness that our lives are moving toward their end, we might opt for denial and welcome medicines that blunt the truth a bit.

Still, I believe it is all of life I must awaken to—the horror, the joy, and the fear. I need to dare to live as fully as I am able. Getting old is not for sissies, we have heard time and time again. Let's embrace that we aren't sissies. Let's take life by the hand. Let's acknowledge that we are not only brave but adventurous, too. Our age need not be a determining factor in our thinking. We can reclaim that the moments when we are fully awake are precisely those moments that our souls chose to experience by taking birth. There is a difference between the dry tea bag and the one in hot water. I don't think we'll know who we are unless we are willing to enter experience fully, however it shows up, and live it with gusto.

Let's remember and take comfort in these familiar words from Psalm 18: *This is the day the Lord has made. Let us rejoice and be glad in it.*

Our Gift

Every one of us has in their being something that is a gift to be shared with those whose lives touch ours. Sometimes the gifts are obvious to others: a knack for leadership, a talent for music, painting, or a calming presence. Sometimes we have no idea what it is that our being offers to others, especially when we are old and can't function as we always used to. This can make us feel like burdens instead of possible gifts to other people. The big temptation when we feel this way is to disparage ourselves. It's hard to realize how in disparaging ourselves we become the very burdens we didn't want to be. Even when subtle, our feelings can fill a room. One of the big spiritual tasks in our later years is to give up needing to be useful as a reason for being. To untether our selves from ideas of what in the past constituted our sense of worth is a bit like free floating in the air. It is liberating when we understand that our worth is not up to us or anyone else to determine. It requires us to trust that having belonged to our Source from the very beginning, we need no longer prove anything.

What a puzzle! When we turn the picture part of any ordinary jigsaw puzzle over, we'll see the brown or gray cardboard backing. No colors. No picture there, just the outlines of the puzzle pieces as they fit together. If we took one piece out of that puzzle, we would surely see the hole it left. On the colored side, the hole left by the missing piece may not be noticed very much, as it may have depicted only a bit of cloud or the green moss on a stone under a bridge, something seemingly peripheral to the main image.

But seen from behind, the absence is very noticeable. Could we prayerfully let go of having to be this or that important, colorful thing and allow our lives to be sanctified by Spirit? When we think we completely know ourselves, we can be quite sure that we do not. It is God who sees the complete picture when we turn ourselves over. Slowly, perhaps daily, we can learn to trust that our lives have meaning in ways we will never understand. That will help us to give up fixed ideas about ourselves and let us live in the ongoing mystery and beauty of daily life with no obvious agendas or goals. It would mean no insistence on having to have things be just so, according to some artificial standard. Could we think of it as an adventure the old can have perhaps more than others? I believe we can freely float in God's vast love without a tether.

afterthoughts

Old inner habits of thought are tenacious. We have inhabited them to the point of identification. They do not have to confine us, however. Residing in a habitat does not define the creature living there. It is still just itself in an environment that might be supportive or detrimental.

To be the specific creatures that we are is what is asked of us, not perfection, usefulness, or any other attribute that our conditioning and circumstances led us to believe we should be.

Spirit is our true habitat and is unconditional in its acceptance of us. That love pours out to each of us. The false efforts of trying to be *of worth* are ones we have a huge opportunity to release. Looking deeply, are we not already of intrinsic worth and belonging to the whole? There is an old and venerable practice we can do that can help train us to mentally remember that we are graced. Crossing our hands gently over our hearts, we may repeat, Wonder-full, Wonder-full, Wonder-full. When we do this daily, a new habitat is created. Eudora Welty said that *all true serious daring begins within*. Then to dare trust the love that made us is a wonder-full practice.

Taking Stock

WHETHER WE WANT TO OR NOT, THERE WILL INEVITABLY COME MOMENTS IN THE EVENING OF OUR LIVES TO TAKE STOCK. What have we done that we are proud of? What have we done that we regret? What has never been resolved? What is there yet to engage in? What has mattered all along?

It's not easy to answer these questions. It's human to shy away from the bare and naked truth. An inward courage is needed to do so, or perhaps we need the truth more than we need the stories we might tell ourselves so that we might look worse or better than we are. When taking stock, we need to smile, to know there is no life without mistakes, without some confusion and messiness, and without sudden things happening for apparently no reason. Nor is there a life without special beauty and hidden tenderness. This is true for everyone.

But deeper than that, it is wonderful to know with our whole beings that we are far more than what we have done or what we have not done. From the beginning, our lives have been held in God's love. Our accounting is not bean counting but counting on God's use of our lives, even counting our mistakes. Then we can trust, knowing that everything that was done by us that we are proud of may be understood to have been done with God's agency. We can drop a sense of ownership and pride and find gratitude and humility instead.

It is a huge relief to drop inflation. Having to be on top, elevated and special, is to teeter on a pedestal whose base always awaits our plunge to the bottom and to the discovery of who we really are: flawed, precious, of singular beauty, and very human. The more we understand and feel God's agency within us, the more effective and beautiful our lives will be and the more they can be lived with delight and courage. This is living in humility. It is a gift of freedom from false efforts and from the tedium of self-absorption. Our given natural capacities will blossom when we act simply and confidently from the love of God within us. There will be a natural quality in what we do. Taking stock with this in mind brings the bar to the heart and not to the striving ego. We can look at the past with genuine, kind eyes that see the grace that was present all along.

afterthoughts

When we can look at the past with kind eyes and see the grace that was present there all along, we will be filled with a quiet joy. It also helps us now, in our old age, to keep growing in the confidence that what we are able to do is enough, even if it is only to smile.

God loves us precisely as we are. To have faith in this is profoundly reassuring. Our precious particularity *does* matter. Our humanity, quirks and all, has infinite value. How curious that in a lived sense of humility so much is rescued. Truth seems always to be paradoxical. Without any self-appointed assessment, we become naked of embellishment. We are stripped of negative self-evaluation. Living then as beloved beings is ultimately both freeing and enabling.

The more we are centered in the fierce, bonding love of God, the more we can release assessment and realize the preciousness of both the difficulties and the joys that are and that have been embedded in our years. Fully consenting to the love that has been and is daily offered to us is the only stock we need to take. To deepen our consent, we can consecrate our cupped and opened hands at the beginning of each day and remind ourselves to take note throughout the day of what is given to us. It is an open-handed gesture, a physical prayer of expectation. At the end of the day, we can take stock of what we have received and give thanks for it. Learning to deeply receive is a one-step humility program. It will keep us growing until our last breath.

Beyond Worthiness

SOMETIMES IT IS HARD TO BELIEVE THAT WE ARE WORTHY WHEN WE CAN'T CONTRIBUTE AS WE USED TO. To open to the truth of our being is to understand that we are God's gifts to God's self. We are not self-made, and we are lovingly invited to participate in whatever ways we still can.

We may wonder, *How can I possibly be a gift while needing so much care and not able to contribute to what is needed?* It takes the aforementioned humility to set this kind of question aside. Our minds can only ask, *Me, a gift?* We don't know how to believe the truth. We don't know what *to do with ourselves.* The answer, of course, is nothing. We do not know better than God, and God made us for God's own to be a gift to God's self.

This is good news, immense good news, and a blow to the separate sense of self with all its convictions. We can only patiently and slowly learn to live like the gifts we were given to be. We can look at a plant and notice that it doesn't ask how or why. It just opens its leaves or petals to the sun and loses them when it's time to lose them. This is completely natural. Sometimes a plant may be dormant, almost asleep, while gathering nourishment. We have times like that as well. Being gifts, we do not need to quarrel with organic, dormant times during our lives. They are necessary.

To accept being a gift is a quiet, internal process. We need to be gentle with it because we are, in fact, shifting out of self-assessment to humble receptivity, a conscious opening where all we think we know goes out the window in exchange for the light that shines directly on us and in us. This is not something words and statements of faith can help us with. Mostly, gentleness is of help, that softening that allows us just to be in God. The mind can't grasp it. The mind actually refuses to grasp it, for it wants to understand in a way that, by its very nature, prevents the ability to have the experience. A plant blooms and dies back, is dormant and blooms again. If we could be this natural, we would experience that virtually everything good and everything difficult is for our benefit. We are so infinitely precious and held in mercy that we can relax even into dying.

afterthoughts

Most of us, when we were younger, wanted to create a mark in the world, to make a difference, and to make something of ourselves. This urge probably continued well into our forties, fifties, and sixties and motivated us greatly. But now we are in another time, when such striving is perhaps not so necessary or perhaps even possible.

This is a time when simple beholding is very important. Our eyes are so very much needed to see and support the younger generation, applauding them when we can. This is a time for gazing at what is near at hand. It's time to fully take in the birds at the feeder, the first crocus in spring like a colorful thumbs-up emerging from the cold earth. It's a time when we can move from hearing to deeply listening.

It is no accident that in the word "hear" is also the word "ear." Usually, when we hear something, we take in information and direction. But when we listen, we use our whole bodies to absorb and be *with* whatever we are with. Could it be that in our older years when we are said to have wisdom to share, we actually have something that is more needed than ever? It is our *with-dom* that is needed.

To practice this being *with* in simple ways can turn out to be a holy occupation. At least once a day, we can focus completely for a minute or two on someone. Doing so, we will make them real. They will feel it. It is precious to be confirmed by someone else's complete attention. What a gift to give and, so doing, we will also continue to grow and become more fully ourselves.

Inner Healing

Many of us have experienced illness in our lives. Illness has a way of assuring us that we will someday not be here. There is no cure for that. In ripening as we age, we can, however, come into wholeness, into healing of our innermost parts. This, of course, has many aspects. We may need to come to grips with unlived aspects of ourselves, with injuries to our sense of self that need tending. We may long to be able to forgive others and ourselves, too. We may long to speak up about something we care about. Life is asking us to live as much of ourselves as possible. What allows us to inwardly heal? Perhaps the most important ingredient is the instinctive and natural urge to become whole. The power of such an inner intent is huge. To come into harmony and peace in our later years is a gift we greatly need, and it is also a gift to everyone around us.

There is a lot of confusion about what wholeness is. Ask a Zen master, a clinical psychologist, a Cistercian nun, a surgeon, a parent, or a clown and they will have different answers. We can perhaps safely say that many parts of us, some perhaps hostile to each other, are somehow gathered into a meaningful and paradoxical oneness. Peaceful and contemplative as this might seem, we also have to accept the crosscutting, tired old saw we sometimes inadvertently are.

Wholeness is dynamic. It is an inner dance of flow and chaos while, simultaneously, deep inside, an inviolate center lives in God's love. It is a center that has never been hurt, will never be hurt, is not required to be different than it is. How many of us will fully feel that or have a relationship with it? Perhaps some of us will, and whether it is fulfilled or not, we can approach that deep longing to be whole with the power of intent. As we grow more accepting of our quirks and foibles, our unanswered longings and blundering brokenness, this center we were given at birth will begin to radiate and incorporate all that once was with all that is. Of course, there is work on the personality level for us to do in order to come into more wholeness. Along with it, and around it, is an opportunity to trust the core where no effort is needed, where we are already complete and can face our death with equanimity. It is a deep trust that we are going home to that which is already home.

afterthoughts

Some of us feel deep anxiety as time begins to run out. My father suffered for a long time with protracted heart problems and the complications that arose from a melanoma that metastasized. He became thinner and thinner. His biggest worry was providing sufficiently for my mother. And often he wondered where his friends were, but having lived all over the world it had been hard to stay in touch with them.

Toward the end he was mainly bedridden. Eventually he was admitted to the hospital, and on the day he died his best friend was fortunately with him. He told us that Father sat up suddenly and with great energy said, "I am so happy." He then lay down and died the next moment.

Something profound had happened to him in the lonely and painful experiences of illness and helplessness. I believe that throughout those last few years he must have reviewed his life. A core place was reached, and he died with unexpected joy.

We have important journeys to make in our last years. Our very wholeness is calling us to accept things that need healing. Something beyond suffering and fear awaits our acceptance. Can we trust ourselves to grow in and through our dark times? It is not only possible but, from a soul's perspective, necessary.

When fear assails us, we can begin to care for it instead of letting it take over. With a little loving imagination, we can hold our fear like a scared child and reassure it, talk to it as if we were there for it with no judgment. The attitude of being the wise elder in our own process is a deep with-dom that will help a lot. It is to be the love that is needed. How amazing to find that we are capable of such self-care.

Holding

HOLDING CAN BE A CONSCIOUS ACT AS WELL AS A ROLE GIVEN TO US WHETHER WE WANTED IT OR NOT. It may have been given to us by virtue of our years and positions. I think of a ring setting that supports a central gem or a seawall that protects a harbor. But my favorite metaphor is wainscoting, that now old-fashioned way to protect wallpaper from damage. Wainscoting is usually made from wood that covers the bottom section of the walls of a room. It is both beautiful and functional. That wood can take scuffs and marring from shoes, bikes and skates that are carelessly dropped against the walls by children.

As grandmother, grandfather, grand auntie, or gran-anything in our families and communities, we are moved in time to the seemingly peripheral role of being present, overviewing and holding from the sidelines what we see. It is a mistake to think of it as being marginalized. We are still part of things and included in significant events but not central in a doing way. Should we not be present at such an event, it is as if something were missing. Our absence can be deeply felt, whereas our presence is sometimes taken for granted when we are actually there.

We can feel sad and confused by this turn of events. Perhaps we dearly wish that we could be and have more of a role. However, ring settings and wainscoting are not nothing! As ones who are holding our families in loving awareness, we have perspective and can see things from many angles. That beholding is a gift we can give. We may feel relegated to the sidelines of family and community life, but we are still very much *there*. And when we are not there, something fundamental would be felt to be missing. Our presence is needed.

Our problem, if we have one, is accepting that we are at the sidelines of ongoing life as we age, even though we still have many good things to contribute. Being metaphorically scuffed and dinged by those younger, exuberant members of our family who take us for *gran*ted is not the end of the world. It happens because we are *gran*-mother, *gran*-dad or just plain *Gran*. They can forget to call us on our birthdays and remember four days later. They may think they have told us how much they love us, but they may have told it out of our earshot. Why not embrace our wainscoting, ring setting, seawalling abilities to behold, witness, and love?

afterthoughts

When we honor the task of holding, we become witnesses to our families and our communities. We are those who have the resilience to let go of our selves and can hold everyone in our hearts and in God's light. By holding on, we are like ring settings for the gems of ongoing life. Taking up this kind of holding is not holding on to scuffs and dings. Instead, we enter into something quite wonderful—the capacity to be truly present to things as they are.

Awareness itself is a gift not only for our own deep growing but also for those who are so much in life that they cannot pause to absorb what is happening in their own living rooms. Could we be placeholders for others? Can we be so present that life all around us can be seen, accepted, and silently blessed?

It is then that we are in the world but not of it. This is a deep secret of inner and outer freedom. We offer our prayer-presence in a time and place without needing reflection in return. Our soul-dependence is not on our family or community but on our relationship to God's love streaming through us. We will have arrived at the place of loving for love's sake.

There we can be schooled to move from attention to careful attendance to what is around us. Even though we may not be of any practical help, we can bless those we are with silently and tenderly. Without grasping, we can hold steady and let God's love flow without hindrance.

Letting Go

How does one let go and still hold? Is this not a spiritual paradox, a lifetime's puzzle? To let go is not necessarily to abandon or dismiss. It is more an inner act of trust. We may feel that we are the very ones, and the only ones, that are needed in a given situation. How, with that conviction, can we let go? We may think that there is no one as able as we are to have oversight on behalf of those we have cared about all our lives. Boxed in by convictions such as these, we won't trust life enough to let it take its course and flow through us and through the situations we are in.

Then, too, our resistance to being helped can make our situations even more difficult. Even knowing that it is we who are creating more difficulty for others in our resistance, we may not yet be able to let go. We feel badly that we are causing stress for others.

There is no magic formula to help this. Sometimes our very age, fatigue, and physical weakness forces us to let go. But that is not really letting go. It is simply capitulation. What can we do? Perhaps a very gentle recognition that we have added suffering to what is already difficult can soften our grip. Gentleness is a tender healer. It is what works best with shock and fear.

Could we practice something simple that is readily at hand? Could we practice exhaling? Since most of us in our last decades have more leisure than in the past, we are able to spend some time practicing being gentle, especially with our exhalations. Every exhalation is an opportunity to let go a little. The more we let go in our exhaling, the more room there is in our lungs for new air. Filled again and again, we are oxygen- and life-infused and perhaps even inspired. This is a constant miracle we can be part of and make conscious. Could we imagine that thoroughly exhaling may start something wonderful we have no idea about? As we practice letting go in small, daily increments, we will become spacious. We will breathe into a sense of *allowing* that is at the heart of letting go. Allowing is not a fight we have lost nor a diminishment we have suffered. It is an enlargement into more being. Even when we breathe our last, if we are conscious, we will know to simply and gently let go.

afterthoughts

As we empty our lungs, there is nothing for a moment. We are in a kind of suspension. We are nowhere and also everywhere. Then life returns with the next inhalation. This consciousness of letting go does often lead us to the experience of being held. It is another nurturing paradox. We are always more cared for than we admit. Could we allow a breath-surrender practice to be at the center of our aging? It turns out that learning to let go and let be is as much for us as it is for others. We might then truly understand that during our whole life we have been breathed and infused by Love itself.

Beginning the day with a few deep exhalations is a lovely prayer practice. It will help dispose us to attitudes and intentions we want to embody. It is letting the out-breath be an act of surrender, releasing what is old, and then the in-breath becomes an opening to receive something new.

We are not *doing* our lives, though we may have felt that we were in the past. Breath by breath, we are being lived by God's love. When we integrate that understanding, it will surely make us more capable of beholding what *is* with love, whether from the periphery or from the center. We are participating in the great allowing that our being born was meant for. We'll continue to be born into more and more experience until we are born into another dimension.

Letting Be

PART OF EXHALING AND THE TRUST OF LETTING GO IS ALLOWING OUR MISTAKES TO BE ACKNOWLEDGED ALONG WITH THEIR LIVED CONSEQUENCES. It is relying on the fierce, bonding love of God that accepts our messy human condition. To actively receive that kind of love is to be revealed in our faults, our hurtful actions, our occasional neglect of others, and our use of them and the misuse of nature.

We don't realize how much of our psychic energy is diminished by our self-assessments and condemnations. Our childhood wounds often keep us from letting love in. We chose distraction, busyness, and even high-minded goals to keep the naked truth at bay and to compensate for things we hid from ourselves. As we age, are we not asked to mellow, to grow in self-knowledge? There is no skipping this kind of knowing in the course of letting go. Through it we enter into the school of letting be. It will bring up a past we often don't want to deal with. Letting be means we have stopped hoping for a different past, as someone unknown to me has astutely put it. There is not one of us who has not done something they regret. There is not one of us who has been consistent with their deepest values.

Allowing this clear admission, we also let go of being the final arbiters of our worth. We let God's Love hold our mistakes and trust that those very same mistakes will somehow be used in ways far beyond what we could imagine. Julian of Norwich wrote that sin is necessary: *It behooved that there should be sin; but all shall be well, and all shall be well, and all manner of thing shall be well.* What a statement of faith!

To allow ourselves to be completely loved means that we must grow in our capacity to let love into those very actions and regrets in our past and in our present that we feel burdened by. This is not something we can do on our own. It is God's work in us. How do we approach this conundrum, then? How do we open to love beyond condemnation and allow it to free us? In a quiet time when we can be alone, let us ask for the courage to name precisely what we did or did not do that we know was amiss: *I betrayed. I miss spoke. I was harsh. I didn't have the courage to stand up for what I believe in. I allowed my own abuse. I retaliated in kind, etc.* The list may be long but essential and humbling in the making.

afterthoughts

Please know that to state these truth-words is a prayer offering. It is a confession that, at the time, we couldn't be or do what we now know we could have done better. We view ourselves without coverup and let the truth be what it was and what it is. We let it be in God's keeping.

Transformation lies deep in the folds of time and even in the darkest shadows of memory. It is no mistake that Bishop Desmond Tutu combined truth with reconciliation. Telling the full truth with compassion frees and reconciles the soul.

Trusting that nothing separates us from the love of God, we can remember a decade at a time of our past. Recalling what was good is an important truth, as well as remembering what was difficult, what we learned, and what we feel we need forgiveness for. It is a way for the years to settle into their places in the past. This can be done over a period of time, little by little. It is well when we have a trusted friend who we can share our life story with. If we do not have such a friend, perhaps a counselor or a member of the clergy could be a respectful witness. Sharing the story of our lives is a very healing and wonderful experience.

However we do it, we can trust that *all* shall be well. Even as our lives move toward their natural endings, we continue to transform, trusting ourselves to God's love, which is vaster than we can ever imagine.

Forgiveness

FORGIVENESS IS A GREAT FORCE OF TRANSFORMATION. It is wonder-full, and it is very difficult, especially if we have been deeply hurt. To come back to our loving selves after deep injury is grace itself, and we cannot and do not do it by ourselves. The passing of time helps us. Love received from caring others helps us. But central to forgiveness is that God is constantly inviting us to return again to the beauty and spiritual wholeness that was given to us from the beginning. We need to let past injuries drop in order to reclaim our spiritual innocence. Our remaining years can be freeing and forgiving years, time for the transforming of old hurts. At some time or other we have all been marked by difficulty. Do we identify with what happened to us, or do we identify with the beauty of our essence? That is a fundamental question, and the answer can only come by consciously living into it. The touching words of Nelson Mandela can encourage us: *As I walked out the door toward the gate that would lead to my freedom, I knew if I didn't leave my bitterness and hatred behind, I would still be in prison.*

We have met older people who have chosen to hang on to what happened that was bad and live their remaining years tied to that tether. They are riddled with hurt the way an apple can be riddled with a worm. Complaint becomes the bitter fruit of their lives. No one can help them, for they do not want help. Their hurt is, strangely, their treasure. Not forgiving becomes a way of being that is filled with seeing fault in others and with years of unlived opportunities for joy. If we were to put it graphically, it is to choose to eat the worm rather than the apple. A healing and courageous act would be to make an accounting of things that we think need forgiveness. Probably we would name ourselves, but that will be dealt with later, even though it is never separate from the task of forgiving others. If there is something on that list that seems to us unforgivable, we must turn the forgiveness process over to God and own that it is too big for us. The other things, however, can be opportunities to metabolize and integrate what we learned and gained in what happened. Did we find out how strong we were? Did the ugly happening turn us to something of more value? This kind of mulling may take some serious digging, but it shows us that the benefit ledger is much larger than the detriment ledger. We recall our memories again but with greater wisdom.

afterthoughts

When something remains that we seem not to be able to let go of, we may have imposed a requirement that the person who harmed us should finally acknowledge that fact, or that the person to whom we have given more than what we ever thought we could should say a true thank you, not a polite or expected one. In other words, we are demanding something. That is not forgiveness. That is accounting.

To abandon our justified longings for some kind of conscious reciprocity is hard work. It's freedom work, for as long as we hold on to our silent, private (or maybe not so private) resentments we hold ourselves away from the great love offered to us each day. Not even the hard work of understanding why someone could not meet us in heartfelt reconciliation will satisfy us. Sometimes we must simply ask for the canker to be left as is. Allowing it to be allows the truth of both our demand and our inability to let go. We need to be honest about this, for truth precedes reconciliation. If all we can do is own our continuing demand for something that can't be given, we keep ourselves in a prison of our own making.

What can we do? We can do something truly beautiful and amazing. We can surround our pain with respect. We can admit its hold on us. We can put some written words about all this in a fireproof bowl. Making the inward process visible in a concrete way helps us separate from it. We let the bowl hold our pain for a time. Exposed to the light, all the longings buried within the pain may erode a little, the way all things left out in nature start to crumble little by little. This way, we slowly let God's love heal us of any self-made troubles. Slowly and gently, a sense of lightness can emerge from within and can be seen in the twinkle of our eyes. After enough time has passed, we can take the contents of the bowl and burn the words or bury them. It will be a comforting ritual of release.

Forgiving Ourselves

IF WE HAVE LIVED AT ALL, WE WILL HAVE A DEEP NEED OF FORGIVENESS. There is no way we will not have been hurtful to someone or something. Sometimes it is much harder to forgive ourselves than to forgive others. Both are necessary and are hinged to one another. Like any door, forgiveness opens from both sides.

At some time or another, we will have caused suffering by lack of attention to others who needed us. We scarcely gave it a thought. We will have harbored resentment and perhaps some small and deliberate acts of meanness. Or by assumed entitlement, we may have stolen opportunities from others. No doubt the list is longer than we want to know.

In our later years, coming into honesty about our need to be forgiven for what we have done or not done to cause suffering is to move courageously toward peace. It is in those steps of naming and owning when we took a wrong turn that the forgiveness process can begin.

To blame others for the way we acted is very tempting. "I did it because of what they did." The fact is we chose to do it. We did it. Other ways we avoid is believing we didn't know. Usually we knew or felt an uneasy something and skipped right over it. It may also have been true that we didn't know, but the hurt happened anyway. We were part of it willy-nilly and bear some of the burden. Desmond Tutu taught the world that without truth told about atrocities committed in South Africa, there could be no reconciliation.

We are not accounting atrocities, but we are accounting in order to know that we know. It is beautiful and necessary. Accounting in which we linger in self-condemnation is a huge detriment. We may then still be indulging in how right we are about how wrong we have been. To allow God's love into the secret chambers of self-blame, self-judgment, and self-hatred is to dissolve a separate self-sense at a primal level. Every avoidance and excuse we conjure up because we still secretly declare that we are not lovable has to melt away. They are the sneaky ways we hang on to being separate and in control. The refusal to be loved precisely as we are and have been keeps us unforgiven.

afterthoughts

Robert Frost said, *Home is the place where, when you have to go there, they have to take you in.* No matter how far we think we have strayed, we really never were anywhere but in God's love and keeping.

The job of self-forgiveness is not one of doing anything. It is one of receiving and accepting. We are and have been and will be dwelling in the Mystery of love always. Whenever we really let ourselves live in that mystery, we can notice what is present in the moment. We don't then see backward or forward. Mystery shuts the doors on any control and planning, on any careful ways we shore up in order to be safe. Mystery belongs to God, and that is where we are remade and loved again and again.

Why not hand ourselves over to living in God's love every day? Before we leave our beds in the morning we can state, *My day is Yours. My life is Yours.* Taking the time to feel those words fully will let them enter us deeply, especially if we do this on a daily basis. In bed again at the end of the day, we can ask for our lived day to be blessed. Then we can ask for rest in God's love. Can we let God's love of us be not only forgiveness for our mistakes, but also God's use of our mistakes as well as God's use of what was positive and life-giving in the way we lived the day?

To allow God's love into the craggy cracks of separation is to be stripped of everything as our own. We know that we are known and that we can never again say that we are unloved. Everything simply *is* and belongs to God. When we experience that day after day, we will be in the greatest of human adventures.

Seeing the Goodness We Are

TELLING THE TRUTH ABOUT OUR MISTAKES IS ONLY HALF OF THE TRUTH. FOR SOME OF US, ACCEPTING THAT WE HAVE BEEN CONSISTENT IN ACTING ON OUR VALUES, that we have loved and given much, can feel awkward. *It was nothing. Anyone could have done it*. We may have been schooled to think and say this.

Why is it so hard to fully accept that God made us good and that we have done good things with that goodness? Undue modesty in this might reveal how little we think of our efforts. But when we are filled with gratitude for what we were able to do and that we could do it because we were given the physical and social resources to do so, we discover that joy is at the heart of the matter. We would be exceedingly glad that God used us. It is a healing thing to name those of our accomplishments of which we are glad. "What a blessing that our children are sturdy now and are on their own chosen paths. What a blessing that we could help this person or that one. How wonderful that we could benefit others whom we will never meet, etc." Thinking this way is not wrong. It is important to celebrate the truth of God's abundant grace that passed through us to others. It is in God's trust in us that we were given the ability to touch others with our lives.

Sometimes superstition invades our joy. If I let myself be happy about me, I will bring on bad things. Better to lie low and say nothing. This is forgetting that God wants us to have abundant lives and to be in joy. We can have lives like that when we recognize that our accomplishments are God's gifts to us and through us. To be loved into joyful action is one of life's greatest pleasures. Why not take thought of one accomplishment we are happy about and look closely at how we were supported to make it happen by the help of others and by God's inspiration inside us? Nothing is ever done by us alone. Looking deeply, we will see that it is always together with others, with circumstances and chance encounters, that things have a way of working out. How reassuring this truth can be when we may have very little we can do now. Then our task in our declining years is to trust that our very being is of holy worth. Messy, limited, broken, loving, good, and glorious, we belong to God. Could that belonging be what we allow at the deepest level? It is a quiet yes and thank you, a celebration and a fruition that took many years to come about.

afterthoughts

Having lived full tilt, can we now understand that Spirit was with us throughout all those years? From this vantage point, we see how we were actually guided when we thought we were simply doing what needed to be done. It is nourishing to know God was there all along and that God is here with us now.

Thinking these thoughts and others like them, however they may come to us, could we sense how we be-long? Could we find again and again that we have been and are be-loved? How continuously tender, then, it is to be in Spirit. That cannot be taken from us. The permission has always been to BE.

We still may have things that we feel inspired to do. We will probably do them at a slower, measured pace. It is amazing how very small endeavors can bring us and others delight. Doing BIG things is not likely, but doing small things with great love is possible. Here's a favorite quote of mine from Helen Keller: *I long to accomplish a great and noble task, but it is my chief duty to accomplish small tasks as if they were great and noble.*

Dependence

THERE COMES A TIME WHEN THE EYE EXAM IS NOT PASSED AND THE DRIVER'S LICENSE IS REVOKED. The keys to independence jingle in someone else's pocket. And perhaps after that, a day arrives when someone else balances the checkbook. More intimately, a day arrives when someone chooses what we are going to eat for breakfast, lunch, and dinner and when we are going to be tucked in for the night. Scary prospects! We will be someone's task. We will be dependent, and that is what *is*.

Contemplating these changes before the day they arrive is frightening. We wish that they will never happen. We may even want to pass away before it happens. Yet, what we anticipate may not be as terrible as all that, for if the eye exam is failed, and if the checkbook is a confusing mess, we might find that we welcome help. Being dependent then might turn out to feel okay. But ahead of time, we don't expect to feel that way.

Thinking ahead, however, we might consider who might be the one we trust with certain tasks that we will no longer be able to do for ourselves. Who will share and protect not only our values, but also what we have of value? Who has treated us with dignity that we wouldn't mind receiving help from? Who is capable? One person may have wonderful fiscal abilities and zero empathy, while another has all the care genes and fails bank book the way a kid fails scissors in kindergarten. We can, of course, just let things happen and not think ahead. The truth is that we've been dependent since birth, or, more correctly, we have been interdependent all our lives. But now a time has come when the balance on the scales has shifted. We might be again as we were when we were little…dependent.

Could we have conversations with key people that prepare for the future? Could we ask those we trust if they are willing to be depended on? This means we are asking to be part of someone else's life and plans. But maybe we can be part of the planning, and that would feel good for both parties. It will be a relief for those who see us age to know that we are not only aware of our upcoming needs, but that we want to be responsible for them as long as possible. We can't plan everything. Things will always change, and grace will also enter our lives in radical ways.

afterthoughts

So much in being dependent is waiting...waiting for our meal, waiting for the ride to the doctor, waiting for the doctor, waiting for a call from a family member or a friend. In dependence, we have to give up our natural rhythm to fit into the rhythm of other people's lives. So, to know someone will truly show up when they said they would matters a lot.

Tolerating, forgiving, and accepting those times when we are forgotten is spiritual work. They are small blows to our ego, and they hurt. We do our best to move beyond the annoyance of it all. To *soften often* is good practice. In it, we relearn to go inside and to find a center of stillness and peace.

As we are able to wait more graciously outwardly, we will be more understanding of our own restiveness as well as of the burdens our friends and family carry on our behalf. Then, to have inner silence is to have a safe place to dwell where Spirit waits for us. We are practicing going home every time we patiently wait.

Nothing is certain except our death. To accept our death is actually to accept our life more deeply. We can kiss joy as it flies, as William Blake wisely said. Living daily in God-dependence, we will grow in gratitude for all experience, dependence in old age being one of them. The deep knowing we come to when we spend time in open appreciation of our lives is that we have always been dependent on God's presence, mercy, and love. Now, in this time of dependence in old age, we can feel it as the ground of our being.

Dignity

Dependent as we might be in our later years, it is very important not to lose a sense of our dignity. As babies we came in *trailing clouds of glory*, as Wordsworth put it. Can we end our lives returning to our source knowing that we trail clouds of glory now as well?

There's a great difference between pride and dignity. Pride is mostly a desperate strut, a demand to be taken seriously or to be given respect when, at the core, such persons are often very unsure of themselves and cannot admit it. Dignity has sturdy ground under it, while pride is a bit like advertising to promote oneself, a shaky position at best. The ground that dignity has under it is reverence for the life we have that was not earned or deserved but a gift. When we truly honor that gift, we will be living in dignity.

Small things can remind us to take care of that gift. Those things will seem quite mundane, perhaps, but will nevertheless signal our worthiness. Washing our hands and our faces as acts of grateful recognition is an example. There we are in the mirror just over the sink. Our faces may be wrinkled, but they are alive and belong to us in the moment. With a warm washcloth we can honor and respect our faces.

It's easy to stay in pajamas all day. Very few people would even know that we did, since visits may be less frequent. Why bother getting dressed? Putting on fresh clothing can be an act of dressing ourselves in dignity. We are living this day not for the approval of others but as a gift given to us. Let us clothe ourselves, then, in grateful recognition of this day.

To set the table, if we can, and invite ourselves to the meal is another place where we can signal that we are worthy and know that we need both the food on our plates and a place at the table. Here's the lovely surprise. When we confer dignity to the tasks we daily undertake, we become dignified. That will be seen in our bearing. We will sense that in beautiful and upright ways, we now elicit being treated with dignity by others. And, as needed, a quiet *no* in the presence of disregard will stand us in good stead. It won't be a loud protest, but it will be a statement visible in our bearing. Clothed in dignity, we will know to be gracious when there sometimes happens to be an absence of graciousness.

afterthoughts

We are here to live, to grow, to create, and to ripen in our lives. We are not here to dominate, which is the hidden energy that lives in prideful people. We will feel our backs go up in the presence of energies that smack of domination. It is the body's subtle signal to take our bearing seriously, to be upright about our and everyone's equal right to be.

We can see, then, that dignity is also about saying *no* in whatever ways we can to being unconsciously mistreated, either by others or by our own hand. It is a stance to be *for* something. When we live in a dignified way, we will know we are for the intrinsic right to be, to express ourselves and to contribute, even if all we can do is smile and say good morning.

It will always be a good morning when we consciously take up living in dignity, for doing so never takes away dignity from others. It confers it, instead, not only to other humans, but also to animals, to plants, and to every form of life. Living that way, we will confirm that our life stories are part of God's vast unfolding story.

Limitations

As we age, limitations will be close at hand. They can be physical, mental, financial, and emotional. To make friends with, or at least have a peace pact with, our limitations is a lifelong process and is ever so much more heightened when we are old. If we approach limitations as if they were friends, we can explore their possible gifts.

We know a sonnet has fourteen lines and keeping within those fourteen lines, the great poet, Yeats, managed to allude to the whole of the Peloponnesian war in his poem "Leda and the Swan." Limitation can be that kind of catalyst. Suppose our walking becomes difficult. Could we approach the distance from the chair we usually sit in to the dining room chair as an explorer would? If we imagined that we were crossing a vast unexplored territory instead of the same old pattern in the rug, we might start to feel differently. This may seem fanciful, but imagination moves both walls and discouragement away.

We could play, What trek will it be today? Let's dream it up over an atlas. Every step can be a mile and will bring us to the dining room table in triumph.

Let's think about plants. Some thrive in pots that hold them closely. With enough rich soil, sun, water, and nutrients, they bloom even in winter. Here is the key to living with limitation. We have the same needs as plants. What can represent rich soil for us? Could it be listening to music or an audiobook? What is water for us? Could it be contemplative prayer or a phone call or a visit from a loved friend or family member? And sun? Could it be staying warm in comfortable clothing and still have a window open where sunlight can cascade down and lift our spirits?

Staying clear of being pot-bound, we need to seek ways we can still contribute so that in other ways we are still connected to the world. Could we dictate or write a letter to a prisoner, for instance? Could we knit hats, socks, and mittens for people in need of them if our fingers are still up to it? To be creative in limitation is to keep on growing, not as in growing old but as in continuing to grow while old. People who care about us will surely brainstorm ways we can participate. We can ask for ideas and support. We can trust that with whatever energy and life that is still in us, we are able to blossom.

afterthoughts

Believing that a contribution must be grand or in some way *significant* will surely stump us. It is in the constancy in which we do what we do that significance abides. The straw that broke the camel's back was only a straw, after all, but there had been millions of straws before that one. Could we be happy to lift one little straw off the poor beast? It doesn't look like much of an accomplishment. But imagine years of daily lifting a little straw off the camel: what would then be true?

Longing for something we can't do puts bails of straw on the camel. A simple act of generosity, love, or courage is not nothing. We can do those. We are never too old to smile, to say thank you, or to ask how someone is. We can choose to be happy. Yes, it is a choice.

If fourteen lines can start or contain a war, then fourteen smiles might prevent one. We will never know what small acts from the heart can accomplish. They are of infinite value. It is how happiness is made for both giver and receiver. The results these acts have are none of our business. But it is our business to continue doing them. Teresa of Avila assured us that *the soul is capable of much more than we can imagine.*

Listening

THERE ARE SO MANY WAYS TO LISTEN. We can listen with anticipation, hoping to hear the footsteps of a longed-for loved one coming up the stairs. We can listen with dread for someone who is to help us, but knowing that the help, though needed, is uncomfortable and possibly painful. We can listen to music and have our spirits lifted. We can listen to the ticking of the clock in the dark when sleep eludes us.

Even when we are hard of hearing, we can listen to our bodies and feel the pulse of our hearts, the rise and fall of our lungs as we breathe. We will be listening to and joining with the experience of being alive. We are wherever we are in a now we can sense/feel/hear. This is an intimate act. Listening in this way, we gain a feeling of spaciousness. We open ourselves to hear our souls speak to us.

Listening, without an agenda and with simple presence, is a wondrous gift we can give to ourselves as well as to others.

When we listen with interest and spaciousness, then shy, neglected parts of us have a chance to speak up. To be received in this way is a miracle and a confirmation of being. Having the experience of being heard heals much. It is as if parts of us, and also parts of others that have held their breaths for years, can finally exhale.

As older persons, we tend to have more time. Even if there are many things we can no longer do, careful listening is something we *can* still be about. Simone Weil, the French philosopher, mystic, and political activist, said, *Absolutely unmixed attention is prayer.* When we listen to each other with pure attention we are in reverence. Being heard in reverence is very rare. It is a gift we can cultivate and learn to give.

We do not have earlids the way we have eyelids, so it is with discernment that we must go about choosing what to listen to. That will require our conscious presence, our willingness, our attention. Listening to silence and to our inner stillness is perhaps the most penetrating of all listening we can do. In the deep chambers of our core, we can hear God speak to us. Learning little by little to value the quiet that allows us to hear Spirit whispering in us is a profound task of growing as we age.

afterthoughts

Listening is not ultimately about sound but about presence. To sense/feel/hear/see the moments of our lives is to be at the birth of time over and over again. Why is it that we seem almost always to sense/feel/hear/see what is painful in us and around us? It must be that pain seems to speak louder than other things. Pain asks something of us. It invites us into the necessity of feeling our grief.

We don't come to acceptance and renewal without periods of grief. There is nothing wrong with grieving. It's necessary and is not easily done without the companionship of another. Joy waits at our side like a faithful puppy wagging its tail for attention. Joy-filled being is not hanging on to grief or grievances. It says, Let's GO. Let's live.

It's today! Joy is built into us, though it may be hidden in hard times. But it will return, and it demands our engagement. Joy and grief are ultimately friends. They make us whole and they ask us to live fully. Khalil Gibran wrote that *the deeper that sorrow carves into your being, the more joy you can contain.*

Time

Now that being busy about many things has slowed down because of age, the trajectory of our lives may be sensed differently. Throughout the different stages of our lives we may have thought we were on a journey and that we had a destination, something important out there to reach or to be about. Having goals and making them happen was very important. Being responsible for spouses, children, and jobs gave us challenges, satisfactions, and a sense that we had a place in the world. We were up to our navels in life and in doing.

Now, more quietly on the sidelines, we may sense something different. We might be able to feel how all through our lives we were also about growing, changing, and experiencing. These weren't goals. The events and the people we were among gave us responsibilities, but also they gave us response-abilities, and it is the latter that have mattered to our inward being. That core being is still growing.

Now we can begin to see that our sorrows and our sufferings, our mistakes and our refusals to care enough are as much a part of us as the joys and star-studded gifts and accomplishments we have had. Thomas Merton, in his book *My Argument with the Gestapo*, wrote: *If you want to identify me, ask me not where I live or what I like to eat or how I comb my hair, but ask me what I am living for, in detail, ask me what I think is keeping me from living fully for the thing I want to live for.* Our older years can be about knowing ourselves fully and honestly. It is no longer as busy a time as before. It is more of a knowing time, a knowing-with-our-selves-time.

If we can embrace the whole truth (though it may feel like herding cats), we may come to have a sense that we have not been on a journey so much as growing and gestating a fuller being. We are human beings, after all, and not human doings. We have time now to turn our faces toward the Love that gave us this profound adventure. Perhaps, in the very soft way that Irish rain will finally soak through a woolen sweater after many days, we can come to sense how much living water we have been offered and how much has soaked into us.

afterthoughts

How many times have we said or heard, *I don't have any time. I'm flat out*? But, of course, we do have time now, and it is high time not to waste it. What are we living for now? So many, after retirement, feel that their lives are over. We no longer know how we can be of use. That may put us in a long period of confusion and of struggle with the loss of being somebody. There's probably no way of skipping this, because self-assessment is a habit that tends to linger on.

What if our later years ought not to be about accomplishment but about receiving and loving, knowing that without having to demonstrate anything we are lovable? We might begin then to explore a day when we could ask, *What does a loved person do in response to being loved?*

It's an excellent question. For some, this may be the first time they let being loved and being lovable in at all. For some, it is time to find a way to love in return. For some, a sense of gratitude begins to fill every nook and cranny the way butter does on a warm English muffin. For some, it may lead to doing something they have never done before.

We can take heart from Isaiah: *Do not be afraid...I have called you by your name, you are mine* (43:1–2). And also in The Song of Songs: *I am my beloved's, his longing is all for me* (7:10). As long as we have been alive, God has longed for us, for the very ones we are. The patience of that Love is beyond imagining. It waits for us without insistence but with persistence. What do we do with our time now, we might ask? To grow into the answer, we might do something that is a little new every day. It doesn't have to be big. It could be as simple and quiet as reminding ourselves daily that love flows like blood in our bodies. We can make a "for instance" list of possibilities and begin to act on them. We can ask for help in dreaming up ways to explore and live more fully.

Loneliness

IT IS WELL KNOWN THAT OLD AGE IS A TIME WHEN MANY ELDERS FEEL LONELY. It's true that every one of us will have been lonely sometime or other. No one can live our lives for us or die for us. This is ours to do, and we have it as a commonality. During bouts of loneliness, that fact doesn't soothe us. Perhaps nothing can soothe us at those extremes of feeling alone. It is an existential experience.

Some spiritual myths posit that God was also lonely and needed creation in order to have companionship. And we, as part of God's creation, have to be free agents so that whatever responses we make are ones that are freely given. There is also the tradition in Judaism that loving acts continue to complete God's creation. That puts conscious response squarely into the picture, doesn't it?

One response to loneliness might be to grab anything that for a moment will distract us from the feeling. We turn on the

TV. We seek activities with other people just to have a sense of others around us. But loneliness may still be there. To work with loneliness is essential, for it can easily lead to depression and illness. How do we work with it since it seems to have a mind of its own? A key is to remember that our minds can fill up with notions that aren't true or are only partially true. We then go on to believe our own constructs and build a greater sense of isolation and abandonment. *No one remembers me. No one visits. I don't count. Friends are scared to be with a person who is sick or in pain or whatever else they think we are.* Some of what we think may be true, but we have made it far worse. In loneliness we see ourselves as separate, and we go about collecting all the mental proofs to make that true for us. The mind is not going to heal the heart, but the heart can do wonders! Paraphrasing the Indian master, Sri Nisargadatta it could be said that *the mind creates the abyss, and the heart crosses it.* Through tenderness of heart, we can move from loneliness into solitude, where we live *with* ourselves instead of apart from ourselves. Being *with* ourselves, there is companionship and hope. In his book *The Awakened Heart*, Gerald May urges us to think of our true home as being God's love. It is a much better place than some of the sad houses we invite ourselves into. What we think is key, but when we let the heart lead the way, our thoughts will change and our lives will be fuller.

afterthoughts

When we are in a state of abject loneliness, we will believe that it isn't only a reality now but that it will be a reality forever. We don't see how we create our future with this kind of thinking. A thought held continually tends to bring about the feared outcome.

Wouldn't it be better to mull a little? "Okay, this is now. I'm lonely now. I've been lonely before and I've survived it. I'm not the only *one in this boat*." Such mulling might bring us to a tender sense of solidarity with those who are suffering the same way we are. There are millions of us.

Could we turn our loneliness into a prayer for the lonely? When we do, we enter a shared and common ache without making a future of it. We will find ourselves in a present and loving moment of compassion. We are no longer all by ourselves. We are in the family of humanity and in God's love. This is when we can renew our willingness to reach out in thoughtful and reassuring ways to others in whatever ways we can. Doing something for someone else is magic. It is the way we mend the world for and with each other a little at a time.

Hunger

SOME SENIOR CITIZENS GO HUNGRY. There is not enough income to pay for food and medicine. Sometimes we might find ourselves dreadfully depleted, and there is not enough energy in us to make even a simple meal. Many of these kinds of hunger are silent and secret ones that are not known or seen by the fast-paced world that just zooms past its elders.

And there are other kinds of hunger: for friendship, for meaningful activity, for a sense of community. We are, after all, social beings, even if some of us are very shy and introverted. More than ever when we are old, we hunger to belong and to contribute.

Perhaps the deepest hunger of all is the hunger our souls have for our Source, for connecting to the depth within us that longs to be fulfilled. That deep interiority is a vast place that, when we accept it as holy ground, is the place in which nothing but God will do. It is there our soul hunger becomes prayer.

It is a place where we are alone with the all alone. At first we might want to avoid it, but the task is to learn to love it and care for it. When we can think of it as we might a piece of untamed nature, a wild preserve, it becomes a place to be valued, not ignored or tampered with. It is a place that is fundamentally not ours but ours to hold open for God alone. The moment we substitute our other hungers for our soul hunger, we will have disturbed our most precious place of belonging.

How strange and wondrous is the paradox that what we so dread, the feeling of loneliness, is the place where God comes to dwell with us. Spiritual hunger is often disguised as other kinds of hunger, even addiction. The pure wilderness where we meet God is natural. It has seasons, sun and rain, wind and calm. It is a state of consciousness where our tent is actually the shadow and shelter of God's wings. What a huge prayer it is to keep our wild God-place open, to preserve it without trying to make it be what our limited egos think it should be. Soul hunger is natural. It is a yearning for God.

afterthoughts

It is possible to be both wild and old. What is the freest we can be with the never-tamed part of us? It may be as simple as reading books about far-flung interests. Or we may take all the time we want in silent contemplation or in sitting under a tree with no inner demand to do anything else. Looking carefully into this, we'll know it is not indulgence. It is giving the unconditioned life in us breathing room and simple ways to be alive.

We don't put a cactus in the Arctic or a tender Alpine flower in the desert. We need to know the inner landscape that lets us feed our souls. Introverts need to be alone to be themselves. Extroverts need interaction to flourish. Those who best know the world through touch can't live in analysis. And the thinker needs delicious mental challenges. What is natural and wild in us wants to live. To grow spiritually while we age is to befriend and care for our soul hunger. It knows what it needs. Can we listen often to the hints that come to us from our hunger and longing and be with them? It is essential to take regular time to enter those feelings, for they are key. It is to be unafraid of the beautiful wilderness inside and to learn to dwell there, where God claims us as God's own.

Old Growth

THE SOUL IS YOUNG AND INNOCENT AS WELL AS ANCIENT. If we had the privilege of experiencing an old-growth forest, a place where humans have not interrupted the ecosystem or the silence, we could perhaps sense something akin in our core. Stepping in from the periphery of a slash cutting where everything is used up, made functional, and expected to be of profit, one steps into an old-growth forest as if over a sacred threshold. It is immediately cool and tranquil among tall, untouched trees. A few more steps and we are enfolded by silence. We become guests, not owners. A sense of presence moves toward us as if from forever and recognizes us, welcomes us, and says, *You*.

The tables are turned. It is suddenly not so much you seeing the forest as the forest seeing you, meeting you with its untouched self. Here, then, where we have no rights of ownership, we are included as if we always belonged here. The trees are not here waiting for anything. They are emitting beauty and silence. The trees are allowing their roots to entwine with the roots of other trees. Their branches reach toward light and offer places for birds to alight and make nests.

This is a metaphor for a soul's sanctuary, of course, but it might help us to imagine and sense what it is like to be free and innocent as well as ancient and knowing. Here we do not depend on thinking. We are being. Without grasping anything, we nevertheless deepen and grow. Our hunger is no longer hunger. Somehow, by simply being, we are satisfied. It seems that persons who habitually place themselves in the precincts of the soul become inclusive and very human toward others. They are living miracles who do not seek attention but instead give attention in the same generous way that an old-growth forest does.

Thinking is not wrong. We need it to manage. It does, however, keep us at a distance from being. When we think, we are subjects that are thinking about an object. There is a distance between us and what we are thinking about. No matter how much we want to close the gap, as long as we are thinking, there will be a distance between us and the subject of our thoughts. But when we enter into being, we are in a fundamental unity with what is.

afterthoughts

We often fill our lives with worries and plans and with emotional needs to be valued as persons, acknowledged, and recognized. It ends up being distancing when we could be rooting down into the holy ground of being and lifting our faces toward the light instead. Then we would deepen naturally and join the already and always.

Why is it so hard to stay in the present without preference? To be able to live like that is to be somewhere specific but also somehow everywhere, too. We can practice. We really can! Practice doesn't lead to perfect but to more practice and then, seamlessly, to a way of life.

Let's take a moment of any day and firmly say, I'll show up for this without a single notion that it should be different. Practicing, we'd soon begin to sense that we are on holy ground, and like a tree or a simple bush (burning, perhaps), we are part of a sanctuary as generous as an old-growth forest. It is a wild, wonderful practice in which our evaluating minds can take a snooze. Our unzipped hearts can revel in the moment with curiosity and respect. We can let the moment play with us.

The trouble with words and the writing of them is that they define when we could be wordless instead, safe and happy without them for a time. Then a rose is a rose and would speak *rose* to us. And a chair could tell us about its ongoing invitation to be a place for us to rest. We could sit down in wonder and gratitude.

Called by Name

WHEN WE ARE NAMED, THE NAME ADHERES TO US. A name is a word, and it could be something that we welcome or that we can be troubled by. We have many names, don't we? Here are some: Sweetie, Honey, Trouble, Stupid, Beautiful, and at times, Wowza! Perhaps You is the truest. Only God knows our secret names and whispers them lovingly when we least expect it. God always says *You* with unconditional love. It takes a lifetime to follow Luke's invitation: *Rejoice that your names are written in heaven.*

Here we are in our seventies, eighties, and maybe even our nineties. As little ones, we may have had nicknames that pointed out things about us that were endearing or sometimes a bit of a tease. It's good to be okay with all that.

In Swedish, the word for nickname is *smek namn*. It means caress name. It would stand to reason that by now, the caress part might be felt more than before. That's a good thing, because we really were loved back then, at least some of the time. Then there are our given names. We may be named after somebody in our family or because a certain name was popular when we were born. That's the name we are stuck with, the one that Social Security has in its files. We answer to that name when it's our turn for something we've been standing in a line waiting for. It's like a tag for a package. It flags us. It will have influenced us whether we like it or not, but it isn't who we are. Who we are is an ongoing secret. We'll have the names that friends give us and the names lovers have whispered to us on moonlit nights between the sheets. And let's not forget our work names: Dr. So-and-So, or Nurse So-and-So, or Teacher, or Artist, perhaps CEO, or Mom or Dad. The latter are probably the hardest ones of any of our work names. Weren't we flat out gaining those names and then living them? What about Nana or Poppy? Those names may be dearest of all.

So, what is in a name? There's recognition, for starters. At some quiet time, we may think about all the names we have had and chuckle over them. We'll probably come to a sense that in our heart of hearts, we are nameless, and yet there is no one like us in the whole world.

afterthoughts

Many of the names we have carried in our lives point to functions we have had or to certain situations we found ourselves in. Being is never a function. If anything, it is a celebration, a lived *hurrah*. Looking deeply, we can see that we are born again and again into new circumstances and new relationships, and for a time that names us. But we never lose the mystery of being named by God.

How do we keep this sense of mystery alive in the humdrum we might find ourselves to be in, whether at home or in a nursing facility? Perhaps prayer on a daily basis will keep the door of awareness open to this self who does not have goals and whose purpose is to live. Irenaeus said that *the human person fully alive is the glory of God*. That's solid permission to be! We should never let anyone or anything take that permission away from us. It needs to be lived and nurtured every day in some way.

Someone in passing may ask, *How are you doing?* They are probably expecting a simple answer: *Doing just fine* or *Doing miserably*. But you are not doing. You are being. In the Old Testament God named God's self *I am that I am*. Being part of God, as we are, it is our secret and truest name, too.

Curiosity

To fully be requires a lust for learning, for discovering things of interest, in other words, to be filled with curiosity. There are many kinds of curiosity, and they lead to different ends. There is one kind of curiosity, however, that leads nowhere. No doubt we have all felt the curiosity of someone who wanted to know something about us as if to borrow and absorb something for themselves. Or perhaps they may have wanted to know something negative about us so they could feel better about themselves. It doesn't take long to sense these as examples of a carrion kind of curiosity. It leads to dead ends. There's nothing alive about it.

The curiosity that has a quality of interested participation is entirely different. Not only are we learning something we didn't know before, but also that interest is experienced as life-giving, not just for us but also for those around us who sense that we are engaged and enthused. We are never too old to be curious in this open-ended way that loves to understand and to experience.

Just think of how our grandchildren glow when we are interested in them and their lives. It's like giving them a big dollop of Miracle-Grow. Our interest takes them seriously, and they may even feel that they are teaching Grandpa and Grandma something. They are!

Think about the way craft persons are curious about different ways to further their craft. They keep wanting to learn. They are not afraid of failing since in whatever ways an experiment might go awry, they are learning something. A curiosity that is not stopped by failure is precious. Let's take cooking as a simple example. A new recipe might be a disaster and an occasion for future family jokes, but when one comes along that's a winner, all the trying from before is now deliciously tucked into every bite.

When our options diminish, it is good to continue to be curious about something. We could take up birdwatching, plant identification, or handicrafts of many kinds. We could be interested in a period in history or the family genealogy. Being curious about ancestors and the family history can lead us to appreciate the highs and lows of those whose DNA we carry. We will sense how our story fits into the larger story of our people. There are so many things yet to explore.

afterthoughts

Think of babies, how they grasp for things and try to put them into their mouths. This is an early stage of curiosity, needing to feel, explore, incorporate, and experience. Later in life we won't be so oral in our approach, though those who are deeply curious about taste will continue that interest in exploring flavors, scents, and textures.

Many older people become curious about spiritual life. That seems to be organic as we come closer to the great mystery of dying. Here a thoughtful and trusted friend or a rabbi, a pastor, or a priest can support us: not by telling us what to believe but by supporting our curiosity around ultimate things. We need to explore and find our own answers to the unanswerable.

Could there be something that has held our interest all along? We touched it, dropped it, and returned to it. This deep draw…what was it? How did it shape our lives? Something was *there*, and it informed our choices. When someone visits us now that we have reached a venerable age, they might ask, *What did you love in your life?* We probably loved many things, but what was it that came from the heart and the gut that we explored and lived in some continuous way?

When we ask ourselves that question, we might sense it was that *something* that lived us instead of the other way around. Coming to a meaningful answer is to have a pearl of great price.

Memory

We cannot change that we are old. We have whatever resources and friends we have. If we are lucky enough that our minds are more or less intact, we also have our memory. Yes, older people tend to repeat their stories as if they had not already told them many times. It can be annoying. Those stories become important when the landscape around us is no longer as fresh and verdant as times in our youth were.

As children, we may have loved dot-to-dot picture drawing. Moving the pencil from one dot to the next, an image would emerge, something we could not have drawn by ourselves. Now, our memories may be a little like drawing dot-to-dot pictures of our past. Some of us can keep our memories moving like a pencil and over time an image emerges that we could not have come up with consciously. Sometimes we can get a cohesive picture, but sometimes we are halted at a place that keeps us curiously drawn to it. That's when we tend to repeat ourselves.

Memory is a malleable thing. We can remember our past, but we can also reconstruct it by choosing to wonder about it. This will take us away from events we may have thought were the only real ones. Why not color outside the lines now when we can consciously choose to recall more of the past? Perhaps the daily and almost forgotten ways we have lived are far more important than we realize. Recalling an ordinary day long ago may bring back a treasure or two. Remembering our children going to school for the first time will be poignant again. Recalling how we went off to work or to homemaking might bring to mind what was there to help form what we have become. Treasuring the friends we once knew who have moved away or passed away, we can feel the gifts that were there in those relationships.

A very lovely thing to experience is when a friend or family member takes the time to hear our memories. The images we're accustomed to seeing may be added to by them in the process of recollection. We'll have been members of many groups and done many things. But in re-membering our past, we also become card-carrying members of our own lives.

afterthoughts

To have a life at all is a miracle. We have been trusted to house and nurture *that of God* in us, as the Quakers put it. Can we come at last to know that we have that holy beauty within us? Do we allow that truth? As the great mystic, Hafiz said, *I wish I could show you / when you are lonely or in darkness / the astonishing light of your own being.*

All of life has meaning: the good, the bad, the ugly, the surprising, and the humdrum. Life is chock-full, and we have lived chock-filled lives. Let's relish that. With a loved one or a careful helper, we could instigate festivities of recall. Let's have little, impromptu parties to celebrate that we were reborn many times in our lives.

Henri Nouwen describes celebrating a birthday this way: *Celebrating a birthday is exalting life and being glad for it. On a birthday we do not say: "Thanks for what you did, or said, or accomplished." No, we say: "Thank you for being born and being among us.... We do not complain about what happened or speculate about what will happen, but we lift someone up."*

If memory can bring us back to accepting and reverencing the present, we have moved full circle. Call it a birthday party or a happy graduation. It doesn't matter what we call it. We are celebrating the fact that our lives have been chockablock.

Passion

YOUNG PEOPLE HAVE NO IDEA HOW PASSIONATE OLDER PEOPLE CAN BE. Constricted by illness or other difficulties, they are yet fully alive...wonder-fully alive. Just think of a plant setting seed in autumn, getting ready for winter. Packed with power, those seeds, when given earth, water, and sun, will break their casings and set down roots. It doesn't matter how big or how small the seeds are. They are pure potential.

It's great when young people can feel the enthusiasm in us. They will want to seek us out to learn a bit about passion in later years. The seeds of our lives are power packed and full of potential, whether on this side of the veil or the other. We need to claim that about ourselves and embrace what we still can express and do.

So much is taken for granted when we are young and agile. To jump out of bed of a morning is nothing, but now swinging our legs over the side of the mattress can sometimes be an accomplishment. We don't take our ability to do so for granted anymore. Showering without help means delicious privacy and the freedom to feel warm water on our skin without being observed. Not burning the toast or forgetting the coffee pot percolating on the stovetop is pure relief and joy.

Every step of continued independence is a celebration, just as when we were small, when every tottering step toward independence was applauded. How much we took for granted in our middle years. We used and misused our bodies. We were flat out in *doing*. Our souls also flattened when we didn't give ourselves soul time. Now, when we can be passionately grateful for whatever we have, we can take up what Meister Eckhart wrote: *If the only prayer you ever say in your life is "Thank You" that would suffice.*

To celebrate aliveness at this stage in life is life-enhancing. Passion is also the ability to suffer with grace. It's a good thing when we take up difficulty and explore how it hones us. It's good for young people to witness us in doing that. Whatever of difficulty we face belongs to us in a mysterious way. It has the potential to make us more of who we essentially are.

afterthoughts

When we don't pit celebration and suffering against each other, we may be able to see how they have been woven together with love throughout our lives. We might then also see the themes we have lived.

In some kinds of weaving, you can see only the backside of what is being made. Inch by inch, the shuttle flies between the woof and the weft. Colored yarn is packed down with the boom. Each day another bit of life has been woven and materializes on the loom. Only later, often much later, can we see the other side. The hard times of our lives allow the celebrations to shine and sparkle. And the celebrations reveal how our difficulties brought profound depth and wisdom to the fabric of our being.

Appreciating our lives this way, we will know in our very structure that everything is passionate, that our Creator suffers, celebrates, and participates with us, weaving love into our days. How extraordinary it is to sense that our passion is part of God's passion moving into manifestation a little bit at a time. To learn a new craft, to study something of interest, to support a young person with our presence and insights, all are ways to keep us living passionately. At any age we can live that possibility. To suffer and to create is one, whole weaving, and it births new life.

Loss and Absence

IF WE ARE ALWAYS CARRYING A FULL CUP, THERE IS NO WAY TO REFILL IT. Convictions and opinions we hold too tightly, past injuries we clutch, regrets we harbor in our hearts, and departures of friends and loved ones we won't let go of make our cups so full of ache that they spill darkness.

Grieving is part of life. At the core of grieving is a sense of having somehow lost a connection to the goodness God put into us. To fully grieve, we transform in many ways. We feel the absence of the one we loved, or the work we loved and lost, or the agility we once had. We need to experience the absence of it. But we can also feel the space that has opened around us. Skipping this is not to live. Spaciousness is near us always. When we are less afraid of the space that a love-loss has left, we have begun to heal. That space may at first seem like an abyss. But that space can also be sensed as the home of possibility when we dare put a toe in and discover that we do not disappear in it.

Another part of grieving is to feel deeply that we have had something we loved! We were gifted with shared time with another or with work we loved or with ways we could express ourselves. These gifts, though they are no longer with us in the present, do not disappear. Nothing of value ever disappears from reality. It is still ongoing and transmuted to other dimensions. To sense the eternal holding of what we once lived and loved is to trust deeply in the vast spaciousness of love itself. We might even be able to know that we are already there in eternity and here with things as they are.

Yet another part of grieving is that we are being invited to enter living in new ways, perhaps simpler, self-compassionate ways. When we lose something precious, are we not asked to find a new, deep connection to ourselves? We need to become the subject of our own heart's care. These words from Meister Eckhart are wonderfully sustaining: *Truly, it is in darkness that one finds the light, so when we are in sorrow, then this light is nearest of all to us.*

Two daily questions we can ask in our quiet times might be: *What can I be about today that will bring more healing and love? What will bring more beauty and closure to this day?*

afterthoughts

The paradox may be that it is in serving others that we may transform our grief most easily. To be in solidarity with everyone who is experiencing what is similar to what we are living is to join the family of humankind. We can then perhaps sense how grieving with an inclusive heart becomes grieving with and for all others in a similar situation. When we bravely take up our own loss for the sake of all others who are grieving as we are, we will feel how that gives meaning to our suffering and transforms it. We will belong to *the all of it*. Then grief will not be the thief of love and meaning but a bridge to a larger way of participating in life and with life.

At Christmas, a friend often gives me an amaryllis bulb. It looks like a lumpy something I wouldn't mind tossing over the hedge. Grief can look like that, inert and lumpy. But as water (tears) and sunlight (acceptance) are given, a green shoot emerges after a time. It is sometimes so forceful you can see it grow visibly.

In a matter of weeks, the red trumpets of the amaryllis are blaring in the sunlit window. There it is: grief turned into something astounding! After a time, the lumpy bulb will be lumpy again. Sometimes we grieve in recurring seasons. Lumpiness returns now and then, but glory is always there. We can't have one without the other.

Gifting Small Things

LITTLE KIDS LEARNING TO GO TO SLEEP ON THEIR OWN OR HAVING TO ENDURE FOR A SHORT TIME THE ABSENCE OF WHAT IN PSYCHOLOGY IS CALLED THEIR *PRIMARY OBJECT*, that is, Mom or Dad or someone truly familiar, may then turn to their teddy with the loose arm or the blanket infused with its special smell. Families sometimes have to make a big U-turn to go to the hotel room or place they just visited because the loved object was somehow forgotten and left behind.

I don't think we grow out of love for some objects we hold dear. They are daily reminders of love given to us by a spouse, a friend, or a child. We see them and hold them for a moment and so touch again a connection of deep value. We all have such significant things in our homes. They help us bridge absence. When we touch or see these signs of love, we might wince because of the distance and loss we may feel again. But it is a sweet and poignant reminder of having been loved.

It is not wrong to think that we will be missed one day. Perhaps giving a particular object to a spouse, a child, a grandchild, or a friend is a thoughtful task in later years. Better to give those gifts while we are still alive so that we can tell those we love why they are receiving what we are giving them.

We are not talking inheritance here. Hopefully, we have taken care of that in wills and trusts along with the needed designation of who will be the executor of our remains and any of our goods that are still left. We are talking about small, love objects that can serve as bridges to memories of loving and being loved. One little thing that may not have monetary value, given from our hands to the hands of those we love, will be a different sort of treasure. Its use and value will not diminish over time. It will continue to be an icon that helps us to remember those we hold dear.

In the process of picking out these things, we will recapitulate years of loving and dear connections. We will touch the uniqueness of each person we are giving something to. We will also remember highlights in our own lives, moments to be grateful for. When we live the process of giving from the heart, we'll discover again and again that only what we gave away is what we truly have.

afterthoughts

Billy will want the same thing as Susan. How do we make sure love-rivalry doesn't escalate because of what we plan to give away? We love each person uniquely, don't we? To pick something special for a person may be a way we can touch both the love and the difficulty we may have had with that person. It will have an emotional value, and where others are concerned, it's never going to be completely fair.

Love isn't fair. It is impossible to love equally. We simply cannot love in a way that can be measured and weighed. We love specifically, and how that love is received is unique also. Every person who was present at a gathering will remember the same event differently. In the end, love can't be grasped. It can only be received.

Love between two people is a little miracle that can continue even after death. In that sense it is the fairest thing we will ever have. And if we have lived it fully, it will remain a cornerstone of our lives. Here's a quote from Hugh Prather that will touch us: *We need other people…to be fully human….to love, to laugh with, to treat tenderly, to be loved by….Unless there is someone to whom I can give my gifts, in whose hands can I entrust my dreams…then I am not human.*

So why not begin, as we can, to pick out things to give away to those we care about since they have been part of the great give-away of love and dreams that's been in our hearts all along. Anne Frank said: *No one has ever become poor by giving.* How true that is.

Permission

THIS MAY SEEM WHIMSICAL, BUT WHIMSY IS A GOOD WAY FOR NEW THOUGHTS TO ENTER ANY STAID HABITS OF MIND. Let's imagine that we have a permission angel at our side. Let's imagine we can hear what our angel is whispering. It might be telling us, *You are young. You still have choices to say "yes" to things or to say "no" to things as well. You can choose to be grumpy or happy. Have you forgotten how powerful that is? There's always something to be learned. By now you are a fine scholar of life. Any setback whatsoever you find yourself in is a place to practice choice. Exactly there, endless opportunities dwell. Right this minute I give you permission to choose to live in a more satisfying way.*

Could anyone think these thoughts without wanting a supportive angel like that? The whimsy of it may make us more willing to try new things. Why not imagine that we are lightly tapped on the crown of our heads with a golden wand? Voilà! You just might be able to feel the permission you still have inside. It may be tiny. But a tiny spark can start a big fire. Or the permission may be larger than you can handle alone. Then permission is to ask for help to accomplish the plans and wishes you have.

We can be the ones who draw a curtain of limitation around us like those privacy curtains in the emergency room that seal us off from others. Then our spaces shrink to the confines of our beds. Let's feel the permission to open those curtains and the windows as well.

We can still have an angel at our side who reminds us that we are deliciously human. That angel will help us remember that being human is about making conscious choices within whatever circumstances we happen to find ourselves. Today, what's the most appealing choice we need permission for? Feeling that we have no choice is a form of dying in the midst of life. It's a good daily habit to feel an ongoing permission to live fully. It will keep us open to the fact that we have choice. Even if what we can choose is small, it will feel good to be able to choose it. Acting on our choices day to day, we can sense how our angel is right there with big, supportive wings.

afterthoughts

"I can't think of anything to choose now," we might ruefully admit. It just seems to be the same old, same old. When we can't get over ourselves, the pity party is in full swing. Hopefully, someone around us will not let us indulge in it for very long.

It is bracing to cast a look backward into our long and precious life. Can we remember something from *back then* that lit a fire and a lifelong yearning in us? The coals are still there. What woke us up to meaning will still be alive within us. We need to give it a little kindling.

How do we do that? It is a matter of claiming that yearning is kin to us. It has been significant in some way throughout our lives. Why not dwell with it in memory or do something small that is still doable? Here it is essential to ask for help to do that if we can't manage alone. We will find it amazing how much help we'll happily get when we choose to be happy and alive again. There will be wonderful helpers, both in spirit and in actuality, to keep our inner fires going.

Just 'Cause

CONTINUING A LITTLE ON THE SUBJECT OF PASSION, A QUESTION MIGHT ARISE. When do we do something just because? We are usually doing things that have some purpose and usefulness. That orientation can spill into a demand for us to *have to be* useful. Don't our actions have to show gain on the credit sheet of life? This way of thinking has a subtle fear behind it. We may fear that we are of no account without being of use in some way. Thinking in that way, our contributions are our right to exist and therefore are considered of value. This is probably not consciously articulated so that we hear it, but it can still be there underneath our daytime awareness. Play then disappears instantly, and being earnest shows up dressed in its starched uniform. Of course, we have a good feeling when we sense we are of use. Yes, there is meaning in serving others. Albert Schweitzer put it well: *I don't know what your destiny will be, but one thing I know: the only ones among you who will be really happy are those who will have sought and found how to serve.* There surely is happiness in giving ourselves. This is not a matter of either/or but one of both/and. It is important to remember that joy is one of the sure signs of the Spirit. To do something completely for its own sake without putting notions of usefulness upon it will give us a break from checking on how we are doing, how we are belonging, and how we are fitting in. For a moment, we can forget about being *good*. It is in the experience of joy that such concerns simply vanish. In full participation with something or someone just 'cause, the veil opens, and we are somehow at home in the *all of it* because we have let go of a tight *me-insistence*. And joy of joys, we are a self nevertheless, still here, blazingly so. No questions asked.

That kind of joy can be explosive, and it can be quiet, too. It may be poignant also when acceptance of pain has turned us around to living fully again. One can't, of course, command joy. *I'll be joyful now.* It doesn't happen that way, but we can be disposed toward entering an event, a task, and a conversation fully. When we continue to release needing our past accomplishments as proofs of self, we may come to feel a childlike delight emerge. We belong to ourselves, to God, to others, and to the world. Such is the magic of joy. It has no why or wherefore.

afterthoughts

Full-blown joy does not pay us a visit on schedule. It has its very own ways apart from hopeful expectation. There are ways to woo it, however. Or let us say that there are ways we are wooed by it. Beauty can do this. It will lift us off any narrow sensibility that we may have been living in too long.

Listening to music, reading a poem out loud, singing, dancing, even if it has to be in a chair, lets our limbs remember freedom. These are ways to wake to beauty. The telling thing about joy is that it always gives us a sense of freedom.

You can't put wind in a paper bag and call it wind anymore. Wind has to move. This is true of joy. It has to prance, dance, hum, sing, laugh, and cry.

When we are older, it may be harder to dispose ourselves to what some would call uselessness. More important now than ever is to give ourselves to something just 'cause, without any goal in mind. Of course, we need to continue to love what we have always loved. That, too, is a sign of joy within us. But why not sing daily any little song we know by heart? It will let us feel our breath vibrate in our bodies and sense a freshening wind in our spirits again.

Shelter

EVER SINCE WE WERE TINY INFANTS, WE HAVE NEEDED SHELTER. Snuggled against our mother's chest, we were nourished by milk, warmth, and protection. Perhaps that is a good description of shelter: protection from harm, warm physical connection, and nourishment.

Whatever our circumstances are in our advanced years, we continue to need shelter. What is felt as *protection* may no longer be a physical snuggle close to someone warm. Instead, it might mean a fierce advocate who will stand up for our rights as senior citizens. What might be felt as warmth might be a friend who will just sit *with* us peacefully without requiring that we be anything other than we are. And nourishment may be just two bites of something decadent we don't eat except once a year at the holidays. Or it may be a warm cup of tea when we are flagging in the afternoon.

Sometimes remembering what has been of shelter to us in

the past brings it back in memory and may lift our spirits on a difficult day. There will have been sheltering presences, those persons who were there for us and did not ask for reciprocity. They were a kind of protection against the cruelty and difficulty that is sometimes part of life. Their presence was a shelter that nourished us with respect, recognition, and love. Looking deeply, we might feel that shelter again and be nurtured.

It is these persons who, in a human way, gave us a glimpse of the shelter that God is. Without those experiences, it is very hard to believe that God is loving and present for us. God's compassion is never not there. It is a fierce, bonding love, and it may take our whole lifetime for that love to be accepted into our beings past our defenses. How dear a practice it is, then, to realize that we can be shelter for one another in small ways. A careful touch might be that gentle force that cracks the Teflon. A word spoken or a silence held might be an opening for someone to feel sheltered. If there are a very few humans in our lives to give to in this way, we can yet give warmth and shelter to a plant, a pet, or a tree in the park. We will become the ones who are of shelter for others.

afterthoughts

No matter how small, no act of love is lost in the universe. An elderly friend told me that she is often awake in the middle of the night. There in the dark, she holds human beings and world issues in her heart, radiating love and solidarity from her small place in the universe. She lets her love flow out to whomever and whatever can receive it.

We do not come to shelter without each other, and we cannot easily come to realize the shelter of God's wings without having felt shelter from a loving other.

How wonderful it is to discover that in remembering how others sheltered us in the past, we become capable of better listening. We also become better advocates for causes we believe in. We are able to feed friends and neighbors and give solace as needed. Maybe sheltering will turn out to be a way of life for us in our golden years. Feeling our capacities, we will inspire others. Sheltering as a way of life may become viral. We are made whole by giving and receiving. It is a central way of being tenderly human together. It is a holy task.

About Being Helpful

We still want to matter. How then to go about it when we really can't roll up our sleeves as well as we used to? Could the very desire to enlarge the territory of those we care about be sufficient? Isn't wishing for another's increased good a kind of prayer?

In wanting to be of help, we can certainly pray that in whatever eagerness to do good things, we do no harm. An image comes to mind of us beached on the shore of questions, desires, and hopes. No matter what, the incoming tide will come and do what a tide does. Later, at low tide, when things are more visible again, we will see what is left.

This rhythm bathes us in salt. Our tears are of the same consistency as seawater. We have tears of joy and tears of sorrow. In trying to be of help, can we let tears fall and not wipe them away but allow them to be shed? We will remember those who rejoiced with us, but we will return again and again in gratitude to those who sat with us in our sorrows and losses without giving any advice. Each must make their own way in life. Another cannot live the life that belongs to us. So, when we try to be of help, can we take back any *urgency* we might have to fix anything and instead ask what might serve ongoing life in the moment? It's good to look deeply at what we say, or do, or don't do, so that the autonomy of the other is always clear and respected. The hardest thing may be to *not* offer help, to let tough things happen when that seems the most loving way. We need to bear the hurt and confusion that such inaction may appear to cause in others. When anyone insists that they are owed something, they are off center. Seeking what we want through constant complaint means that we have somehow skipped the inner work of growing up. It is as if we were secretly saying, *I don't trust myself, so you have to make up for that for me*. This pushes people away. It has to!

The tide returns, of course. The beach is scoured. The cast-up stones are rounded a little more, as are we. Love will ask us to live as fully as possible and to not skip the lessons that are ours to learn.

afterthoughts

If only I had done such and such. If only such and such had not occurred. Our minds can spin in their hamster wheels of regret and the hope for a different past. A deep sigh of recognition is needed. Loss will be part of every life. Connection and constancy in care will also be there. We might well ask, *What is enough?* Is it not to have been given life and to have fully lived it in whatever ways we could?

In trying to be helpful, we can know that to be a witness, to see and speak of another's gifts, is never amiss. We can mirror them without adding or detracting anything. Our best bet is to confirm the capacity of someone else rather than to rush into helping. We need to wait, to hear requests for help, and to refrain when we are not asked.

It is never wrong to wait upon love, to be close at hand, but, like a good waiter, to not go and get anything until a patron places an order. We know a hovering waiter is truly annoying. A cautious distance is needed, as is offering a soulful awareness that is respectful, courteous, and trusting in the capacities of the one whose suffering we want to alleviate.

A little step backward in any eagerness to help is salutary. It will give us breathing room, allowing the situation to have a small respite from having to be solved NOW. This little step is an act of both trust and respect. As we wait upon God, we somehow also wait upon each other. We learn again that love does not belong to us but that we belong to it. And as Julian of Norwich reassured us, *all shall be well.*

In Awe

Awe is surely different from fear yet may be felt deeply in the gut and may make us completely breathless. Our bodies behave similarly in fear. Surely by this age we have felt fear as something familiar that sometimes lurks in the background. Next to our fear reactions, wouldn't it be salutary to embrace wonder instead, to really see how amazing life continues to be?

If we lose the capacity for awe, we have lost something precious that is deeply human. A dear friend of mine shared the words of wisdom that she told her almost-adult son. This is what she said: *Be in constant awe and try to be helpful.* Doesn't that immediately remind us of the first two commandments? *Love the Lord your God with all your heart and with all your soul and with all your mind and with all your strength.* And we know the second injunction: *Love your neighbor as yourself.*

The blessing is that we lose our sense of self in awe and

wonder. It is, in fact, a prayer of adoration. Something of grandeur takes our breath away. We are in a moment of worship, caught in beauty, amazement, gratitude, and reverence. Our souls are nourished. We might not be in Technicolor awe all of the time, but we can develop the habit of noticing, of really noticing, and so be in frequent wonder. As wisdom elders, we have more time for this than we did when we were younger. That gives us the opportunity to discover the infinite layers that are inherent in a simple thing such as tasting, for instance. Let's take applesauce as an example. Not only is it naturally sweet, but also if we let ourselves be nourished at the level of awe, we might sense apple blossoms opening in spring, the warm air and sun of July and August, and the slow ripening of the fruit in September. In one bite we might taste an entire summer as well as early fall. We'd also know that just like apples turning red, we, too, are ripening. There can be so much awe in a little taste of plain applesauce and also in everything we take time to deeply experience.

Everything in life has layers and magnitude if we let ourselves be open to what is right there under our noses. Then fear has less chance with us, for we will be in amazement instead.

afterthoughts

The thing about awe and wonder is that it is participatory. It doesn't let us be spectators. In awe, we don't wonder at something or about it. We are not asking endless whys. Do we ask a rose why it is so beautiful? NO. We enjoy and are enraptured by it. We relate to it with reverence, and that is close to prayer.

On any ordinary morning, we could intend to be open to amazement. Turning toward awe is to intend to be more like a child. Old age and childhood have much in common; feelings of helplessness, of course, but more an unquestioning sense of things just being right and interesting as they unfold.

Do you know that old song, *Picking up paw-paws; put 'em in a basket*? In awe, we pick up wonder-full things and tuck them into the basket of our rib cage and then into our hearts. In every moment of childlike wonder, we reclaim some essence of ourselves, for we are then in life without trying to possess anything but open instead to what is at hand. We'll see the burning bushes where before there were shrubs with long, Latin names. Without grasping for control, we lean toward the feeling of belonging in some tender, almost heartbreaking way.

Actor Reginald Stewart observed that *years wrinkle the skin but to give up wonder wrinkles the soul*. When we feast on wonder, don't we automatically become wonder-full?

Now

It's always all now. Every moment of our lives has been a now. Reading this you are in a *now*, this very moment. The discovery that sufficiency is in the present is to experience being graced. In this our now, all of time is present: our past, our present, and our future. We come home in life when we assimilate all of the goodness of our lives into the present. The goodness and the sufficiency are there. Are we somewhere else? Then let's hurry and come back home to God's now.

There we can surrender our unfinished business. Each of us has unfinished business to place in God's mercy. In this, our present now, we can offer up our strengths and triumphs and efforts. They can all be together, at home, in God's time. We can offer up our helplessness and our brokenness, too. They are all held in God's time.

Even as old as we are, we can trust ourselves to let go of outcomes and move closer to our source and be at home there.

What we have sought has also sought us. The true goal of our lives is within us here and present now. It is to be with our life's Source and live our uniqueness for God. All else follows.

The mystery of sensing that we will soon go home is that we discover we've been home all along without fully knowing it. We already are in everything and belong in it and with it.

Can we sense that our lives have actually been living prayers? They have been full of praise, of suffering, of effort, of sorrow, and of delight. No one has been this particular prayer before. This time in our lives is the Amen time. It is knowing what we know while growing into more awe and more gratitude.

Now is understanding that in every part of our lives, we were exactly where we were meant to be so as to experience and to unfold. That's currently true as well. Can we be accepting that we are where we are meant to be? In this, our here and now, we can emanate love and presence to others from the source of love we have received. It's not really doing anything. Our golden years are meant to be God's gold shared and poured out of us until our last breath.

afterthoughts

There may come a time when we can no longer sustain a conscious connection to the love of God. But if we have practiced *going home* enough, our being will still emanate the love we have received over a lifetime.

Now is a time of recollection and of surrendering what is no longer relevant. As we age, we have an opportunity to move deeper into simplicity. Ultimately, that means acceptance of where we are and the permission to unfold as we still can.

We will sense that the grace that has been given to us is not offered to us as some strange, unfamiliar wisdom, but as a way to help us live the wisdom that has come to be born in us. We have come to these years with grace. They have been a gift, a path, and a long unfolding.

Now is a time we can be born into a deep sense of presence, into the heart of love that birthed us, infused us, and has carried us to this moment, this time of growing into ripeness and fulfillment.

last words

Many of us sense how time is beginning to run out. Some nights my mother would call in abject fear from Portugal, where she lived alone. Yet, before I went to bed on the night she died, I was with her. I saw a beautiful light around her. "Mother, you are so beautiful," I said. She replied, "I have the glory in me." It was amazing to hear. Something profound had happened to her in the lonely and painful experiences of anxiety and fear that she had suffered. I feel sure that throughout those last years, she was reviewing her life. She didn't distance from her suffering. She allowed it, finally. A core place was reached, and she died with glory inside her on the eve of All Saints' Day. No one will ever know the mystery of what had happened for her and in her.

For me, this is living proof that we have important journeys to make in our last years. Our very wholeness is calling us to accept things that are fearful and yet healing. Something beyond suffering and fear awaits our acceptance. Can we trust ourselves to it? To grow in and through our dark times is not only possible but, from a soul perspective, necessary. That is perhaps more true of our good times as well.

We find our homes, build our careers, build important connections, but we can only grow our lives. All that we have ever built stops sometime. Those things have had their time, but our lives go on, sometimes in sunlight and sometimes in shade. Some inner act of growth is still being asked of us. Was there at the outset of our lives a hidden contract we were meant to meet? What is the fruit of having lived? *Ripeness is all*, said Edgar in *King Lear*.

But growing is not in our control. It is a mystery, an amalgam of energy, hope, values, losses, despair, surprises, and amazing gifts. We can't build mystery. We can only participate in it. In life we are borne, as in carried and as in given birth to. Our older years are years when we can value the sheer gift of having lived. I have been so reassured by some sayings of Hokusai that I first read on a wall at the Santa Sabina retreat center in San Rafael, California. I hope they speak to you, too. He says, *Look forward to getting old…you just get more of whom you really are.* And later, he says, *Don't be afraid. Don't be afraid. Love, feel, let life take you by the hand. Let life live through you.*

To *soften often* in this, our last season, is to melt into reverence for life itself. We will never completely know when we were agents of help to others, when we hurt someone without intent, nor will we fully know what grace was the fulfillment of our being. We may have hints about that, though not the whole picture. But we can still cherish the days we wake up in both senses of the word, the days we sense holiness surrounding us and realize that we have never been alone in our suffering. God has suffered with us. May we always keep growing in love, in respect, in gratitude, and in surrender. May our days fill with the joy that is inclusive of the *all of it*.

I began this book with the story of the hydrangea tree. I want to continue the story a bit further. As I related before, the tree was taken to the back of the woodlot. Cut in three large pieces, it was piled up into a great mound. The branches leaned in and became a latticework of twigs. It was a tangled heap left to decompose while being a generous shelter for birds, chipmunks, and voles.

Can you mourn a tree? Yes. I missed that tree deeply. Every once in a while, I'd go and inspect what was happening there in the silent woods. Over several winters, the mound sank and became so integral to the place that it felt as if it had always been there. I could pass it without much thought. But one day I paused in one of my loops through the woods. It was spring. The wild geraniums were in bloom. There was a wet, sweet scent in the air.

Suddenly there was rustling. Out of the mound bounded a little rabbit that I must have scared. It leaped away, and my startled heart took its time to settle down. When I walked closer to the mound to inspect it further, there, growing from one of the branches that had somehow taken root, a single leaf had unfurled. It was a vibrant green, a sign of new life.

We don't know if our lives continue after death. Perhaps they do on another plane. But something green, some new leaves will somehow show up on this side of the veil or on the other. I am convinced of it. There won't be explanations. There will be exclamations! If we served life as we lived it, life will surely continue in some loving and mysterious way.

"In the end, only three things matter; how much you loved, how gently you lived, and how gracefully you let go of things not meant for you."

ATTRIBUTED TO BUDDHA

ALSO BY GUNILLA NORRIS

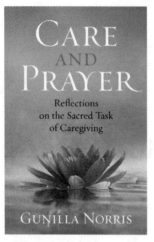

Care and Prayer
Reflections on the Sacred Task of Caregiving

Gunilla Norris reminds us that the daunting task of caregiving is a sacred and holy task, even amid the often-grueling work involved, and that God is present through it all. Suffused with real-life wisdom and deep spirituality, *Care and Prayer* is a light-filled companion for full-time caregivers or anyone involved in caring for another.

96 PAGES | $12.95 | 5½" X 8½"
9781627855662

Great Love in Little Ways
Reflections on the Power of Kindness

Is there anything more needed in our world today than kindness? In this little gem of a book, Gunilla helps us learn to cultivate kindness in all aspects of our daily lives—upon waking to the sunshine, through our work and daily bread, when offering a safe space to a friend.

64 PAGES | $12.95 | 5½" X 8½"
9781627854290

TO ORDER CALL 1-800-321-0411
OR VISIT WWW.TWENTYTHIRDPUBLICATIONS.COM

TWENTY-THIRD PUBLICATIONS
A division of Bayard, Inc.